THE WAY OF THE CROSS
Map Tourist

Enabling readers to walk in Christ's footsteps
in the actual locations via online web maps.

By *St. Alphonsus Liguori*
With map information written by Emmanuël DeWeg

*The book's body text is in the public domain. Please copy, replicate,
and distribute freely for non-commercial purposes to further walking in Christ.
All images are in the public domain and sourced from Wikipedia.*

Feedback about this edition may be provided at Innovativeeggz.com

~ ※ ~

Introduction

Current online maps allow us to walk where Jesus walked while exploring the region's current life through images of restaurant food, grocery store prices, and other historical or current points of interest.

Copyright protections prohibit the posting of the actual images from reviews on websites, so this book guides the user to specific map points from which readers can launch their own explorations.

The result is (once again) confirmation that Jesus walked with us, splitting human history into periods before and after His coming.

Technology

Maps available from any website will work for this book. By zooming in and out, the maps show more or less details and points of interest which can and should be clicked on to explore *your* interests. Some have a view from the street, like Microsoft's Streetside and Google's Street View, which give a very personal feel and are accessible by placing a figure over highlighted areas of the map. While any map software will work for this book, Google's maps are suggested since, as of 2022, they have the most map-linked pictures around the world.

Phones and laptops can project these images to large televisions, called 'casting' or 'screen mirroring'. Projecting allows one person to act as a tour guide to a family or group, and is a lot of fun as participants yell out what *they* want to see.

Technology is ever changing, so for current instructions and troubleshooting, search online for your model and functional needs.

About the Authors

St. Alphonsus Liguori (1696-1787) spent his life on behalf of Christ, writing over 100 treatises and hymns while working with the poor in the streets. His most popular work today is *Uniformity With God's Will* (ISBN 9781640323254) which covers union with Jesus Christ in all that we do.

Emmanuël DeWeg is a pseudonym meaning "God with us" and "is the Way" from Matthew 1:23 and John 14:6. The author's hope is that we all live in God's righteousness and yield our hearts to Him.

Monogram of Christ (Chi Rho), 4th-century AD

THE STATIONS OF THE CROSS
According to the Method of
ST. ALPHONSUS LIGUORI

PREPARATORY PRAYERS

Let each one, kneeling before the high altar, make an Act of Contrition, and form the intention of gaining the indulgences connected to this devotion, whether for himself or for the souls in Purgatory.

ACT OF CONTRITION

O MY GOD, I am heartily sorry for having offended Thee, and I detest all my sins because of Thy just punishments, but most of all because they offend Thee, my God, Who art all-good and deserving of all my love. I firmly resolve, with the help of Thy grace, to sin no more and to avoid the near occasions of sin. Amen.

Following the act of contrition say:

MY LORD JESUS CHRIST, * Thou hast made this journey to die for me with love unutterable; * and I have so many times unworthily abandoned Thee; * but now I love Thee with my whole heart, * and because I love Thee, * I repent sincerely for having ever offended Thee. * Pardon me, my God, * and permit me to accompany Thee on this journey. * Thou goest to die for love of me; * I wish also, my beloved Redeemer, * to die for love of Thee. * My Jesus, * I will live and die always united to Thee. *

FIRST STATION

Jesus Is Condemned to Death

V. We adore Thee, O Christ, and we praise Thee, *(Genuflect)*
R. Because by Thy holy cross Thou hast redeemed the world. *(Rise)*

Priest:

CONSIDER THAT JESUS, after having been scourged and crowned with thorns, was unjustly condemned by Pilate to die on the cross. *(Kneel)*

All say:

MY ADORABLE JESUS, * it was not Pilate, * no, it was my sins, that condemned Thee to die. * I beseech Thee, by the merits of this sorrowful journey, * to assist my soul in its journey towards eternity. * I love Thee, my beloved Jesus; * I love Thee more than myself; * I repent with my whole heart of having offended Thee. * Never permit me to separate myself from Thee again. * Grant that I may love Thee always, * and then do with me what Thou wilt. *

Our Father. Hail Mary. Glory Be.

V. Lord Jesus, crucified,
R. Have mercy on us!
(Rise)

Stabat Mater dolorósa
Juxta crucem lacrymósa
Dum pendébat Fílius.

At the cross her station keeping
Stood the mournful Mother weeping,
Close to Jesus to the last.

First Station Map Tourist
Jesus Is Condemned to Death

Background: The Way of the Cross, Way of Suffering, or Via Dolorosa, is a physical path in Jerusalem for believers to trace, pause, and reflect at fourteen stations on what Jesus did for all of us, at the believed locations *where these events actually happened*. This memorial was performed as far back as the 500s, with station locations changing regularly up to the 1800s. Archeological discovery and Pope John Paul II offering the *Scriptural Way of the Cross* (adhering exactly to Bible verses) may again change the station locations in Jerusalem, but changing stations will never change our need to reflect on the sacrifice of Jesus.

Following the Liguori stations, Pilate asks Jesus if He is king (Matt. 27:11, Mark 15:2, Luke 23:3, John 18:33) and Jesus confirms Pilate's statement. In John 18:38 Pilate asks the question we all seek: "What is truth?" Jesus points to Himself as the answer in John 14:6, "I am the way, the truth, and the life." No answer satisfies Pilate or the crowds, and Jesus is condemned to death by crucifixion.

Location to Search: This first station is on the ramp leading to the door of the "Omariya School Jerusalem" or search these coordinates: 31.7803672, 35.233846

Other Points of Interest: Just south is the Dome of the Rock, a focal point for Jews, Christians, and Muslims. The Rock is considered to be Mount Moriah where Abraham went with his son Isaac in Genesis 22:14, and also where Solomon later built his Temple of 2 Chronicles 3:1.

SECOND STATION

Jesus Is Made to Carry His Cross

V. We adore Thee, O Christ, and we praise Thee, *(Genuflect)*
R. Because by Thy holy cross Thou hast redeemed the world. *(Rise)*

Priest:

CONSIDER THAT JESUS, in making this journey with the cross on His shoulders, thought of us and offered for us to His Father the death that He was about to undergo. *(Kneel)*

All say:

MY MOST BELOVED JESUS, * I embrace all the tribulations that Thou hast destined for me until death. * I beseech Thee, * by the merits of the pain Thou didst suffer in carrying Thy cross, * to give me the necessary help * to carry mine with perfect patience and resignation. * I love Thee, Jesus, my love; * I repent of having offended Thee. * Never permit me to separate myself from Thee again. * Grant that I may love Thee always, * and then do with me what Thou wilt. *

Our Father. Hail Mary. Glory Be.

V. Lord Jesus, crucified,
R. Have mercy on us!
(Rise)

Cujus ánimam geméntem,	*Through her heart, His sorrow sharing*
Contristátam et doléntem	*All His bitter anguish bearing,*
Pertransívit gladius.	*Now at length the sword has passed.*

Second Station Map Tourist
Jesus Is Made to Carry His Cross

Background: Back in Matthew 16:24, Jesus says in order to be His disciple, we must deny ourselves and take up our cross. Here now in John 19:17 Jesus shows us through His example what this truly means. Paul explains further, that when we unite with Christ in His crucifixion (Romans 6:5), we also join His resurrection and life! (Galatians 2:20)

Location to Search: This second station is intended to be located in the foyer of what was Herod's Palace, where Pilate stayed and judged Jesus. This second station is only a few steps away from the first station, on the outer wall of the current "Church of the Condemnation" or search these coordinates: 31.7803473, 35.2336873

Due to current excavations being compared with the historic writings by Philo of Alexandria and Flavius Josephus, it is now thought that Herod's Palace is under the Tower of David, with Roman flagstone evidence viewable at the Tower of David museum.

Other Points of Interest: Also famous at this point is the Ecce Homo Arch, thought at one time to be where Pilate says in John 19:5, "Behold the Man!" or in Latin, "Ecco Homo," except we now know that the arch was built after 117 AD, too late for Pilate.

THIRD STATION

Jesus Falls the First Time

V. We adore Thee, O Christ, and we praise Thee, *(Genuflect)*
R. Because by Thy holy cross Thou hast redeemed the world. *(Rise)*
Priest:

CONSIDER THIS FIRST FALL OF JESUS under His cross. His flesh was torn by the scourges, His head crowned with thorns, and He had lost a great quantity of blood. He was so weakened that He could scarcely walk, and yet He had to carry this great load upon His shoulders. The soldiers struck Him rudely, and thus He fell several times in His journey. *(Kneel)*

All Say:

MY BELOVED JESUS, * it is not the weight of the cross, * but of my sins, * which has made Thee suffer so much pain. * Ah, by the merits of this first fall, * deliver me from the misfortune of falling into mortal sin. * I love Thee, O my Jesus, with my whole heart; * I repent of having offended Thee. * Never permit me to offend Thee again. * Grant that I may love Thee always, * and then do with me what Thou wilt. *

Our Father. Hail Mary. Glory Be.

V. Lord Jesus, crucified,
R. Have mercy on us!
(Rise)

O quam tristis et afflícta
Fuit illa benedícta
Mater Unigéniti!

Oh, how sad and sore distressed
Was that Mother highly blessed
Of the sole-begotten One!

Third Station Map Tourist
Jesus Falls the First Time

Background: The devotional walk continues in the footsteps of Jesus. After Jesus was flogged to a weakened state in John 19:1-3, He was tried and convicted by Pilate, taken out, made to carry His own 120+ lb. cross (John 19:17), and from the cross's weight and His own exhaustion, tradition holds that Jesus fell.

Location to Search: This third station was moved in the last few years. It may be on different maps at different locations. Some maps have it as "Church of Our Lady of Sorrows, Jerusalem," and others "Church of St. Mary of Agony, Jerusalem." The easiest option is to search these coordinates: 31.7799333, 35.2320671

Other Points of Interest: Just behind this spot is the Basti Restaurant & Café, where with photo reviews and menu images, one can see that the locals are indulging in a *tuna* pizza for only $10 US dollars (35 Israeli new shekels in 2019).

FOURTH STATION

Jesus Meets His Sorrowful Mother

V. We adore Thee, O Christ, and we praise Thee, *(Genuflect)*
R. Because by Thy holy cross Thou hast redeemed the world. *(Rise)*

Priest:

CONSIDER THE MEETING of the Son and the Mother, which took place on this journey. Jesus and Mary looked at each other, and their looks became as so many arrows to wound those hearts which loved each other so tenderly. *(Kneel)*

All Say:

MY MOST LOVING JESUS, * by the sorrow Thou didst experience in this meeting, * grant me the grace of a truly devoted love for Thy most holy Mother. * And Thou, my Queen, * who wast overwhelmed with sorrow, * obtain for me by thy intercession * a continual and tender remembrance of the Passion of Thy Son. * I love Thee, Jesus, my love; * I repent of ever having offended Thee. * Never permit me to offend Thee again. * Grant that I may love Thee always, * and then do with me what Thou wilt. *

Our Father. Hail Mary. Glory Be.

V. Lord Jesus, crucified,
R. Have mercy on us!
(Rise)

Quae moerébat, et dolébat,	*Christ above in torment hangs*
Pia Mater dum vidébat	*She beneath beholds the pangs*
Nati poenas ínclyti.	*Of her dying, glorious Son.*

Fourth Station Map Tourist
Jesus Meets His Sorrowful Mother

Background: At the fourth station Jesus meets His mother Mary, blessed among women (Luke 1:42). As sorrowful as Mary was, it is the love of Jesus that was recorded as He secured her protection and provision by assigning John to her as her son (John 19:26). At all times, God is love (1 John 4:16).

Location to Search: This fourth station is on the same portion of street as the third. Some maps have it as "Church of Our Lady of Sorrows, Jerusalem," and others "Church of St. Mary of Agony, Jerusalem." The easiest option is to search these coordinates: 31.7799333, 35.2320671

Other Points of Interest: If you want to take a break from Via Dolorosa and visit modern Jerusalem, Machaneh Yehudah Market, Agripas St 90, has supplies for every traveler, like candy, coffee, and spices. Explore the photo reviews for the latest in Israeli tastes.

To translate the Hebrew words in the market photos with the Google Translate app, point your phone camera at the words on the screen and the app will do its best to translate Hebrew words into English.

FIFTH STATION

Simon Of Cyrene Helps Jesus to Carry His Cross

V. We adore Thee, O Christ, and we praise Thee, *(Genuflect)*
R. Because by Thy holy cross Thou hast redeemed the world. *(Rise)*

Priest:

CONSIDER THAT THE JEWS, seeing that at each step Jesus, from weakness, was on the point of expiring, and fearing that He would die on the way, when they wished Him to die the ignominious death of the cross, constrained Simon the Cyrenian to carry the cross behind Our Lord. *(Kneel)*

All Say:

MY MOST SWEET JESUS, * I will not refuse the cross as the Cyrenian did; * I accept it, I embrace it. * I accept in particular the death that Thou hast destined for me, * with all the pains which may accompany it. * I unite it to Thy death;*I offer it to Thee. * Thou hast died for love of me! * I will die for love of Thee, and to please Thee. * Help me by Thy grace. *I love Thee, Jesus, my love; * I repent of having offended Thee. * Never permit me to offend Thee again. * Grant that I may love Thee always, * and then do with me what Thou wilt. *

Our Father. Hail Mary. Glory Be.

V. Lord Jesus, crucified,
R. Have mercy on us!
(Rise)

Quis est homo qui non fleret	*Is there one who would not weep*
Matrem Christi si vidéret	*Whelmed in miseries so deep*
In tanto supplício?	*Christ's dear Mother to behold?*

Fifth Station Map Tourist
Simon Of Cyrene Helps Jesus to Carry His Cross

Background: One of the many confirmations of biblical truth are the specific details. Here, Simon, from Cyrene, whose father was Rufus (Mark 15:21, Matt. 27:32) could be validated by contemporaries. Simon, though he was just passing through, was seized by soldiers to carry the cross of Christ (Luke 23:26). Learning from this devotion, let us strive to carry our cross in life *voluntarily* (Mark 8:34).

Location to Search: The streets are getting narrower and the vendors increasing, making this fifth station easy to miss. The fifth station marker is on the "Chapel of Simon of Cyrene" though the location is more recognized in maps by searching the Jewish school next door called "Ateret Cohanim Yeshiva" or search these coordinates: 31.7796174, 35.2323673

Other Points of Interest: There is a brown rock in a framed square to the right of the Chapel of Simon door. Here, tradition holds that Jesus placed His hand, and thousands of pilgrims have since done the same.

If in a lighter mood exploring this location, the map tourist can use the pictures posted in reviews and Street View to read the tourist trap t-shirts, or virtually enjoy the food at the "Abu Shukri, Jerusalem" restaurant.

SIXTH STATION

Veronica Wipes the Face of Jesus

V. We adore Thee, O Christ, and we praise Thee, *(Genuflect)*
R. Because by Thy holy cross Thou hast redeemed the world. *(Rise)*
Priest:

CONSIDER THAT the holy woman named Veronica, seeing Jesus so afflicted and His face bathed in sweat and blood, presented Him with a towel, with which He wiped His adorable face, leaving on it the impression of His holy countenance. *(Kneel)*

All Say:

MY MOST BELOVED JESUS. * Thy face was beautiful before, * but in this journey it has lost all its beauty, * and wounds and blood have disfigured it. * Alas! my soul also was once beautiful, * when it received Thy grace in Baptism; * but I have disfigured it since by my sins. * Thou alone, my Redeemer, * canst restore it to its former beauty. * Do this by Thy Passion, O Jesus. * I repent of having offended Thee. * Never permit me to offend Thee again. * Grant that I may love Thee always, * and then do with me what Thou wilt. *

Our Father. Hail Mary. Glory Be.

V. Lord Jesus, crucified,
R. Have mercy on us!
(Rise)

Quis non posset contristári,	*Can the human heart refrain*
Christi Matrem contemplári	*From partaking in her pain,*
Doléntem cum Fílio?	*In that Mother's pain untold?*

Sixth Station Map Tourist
Veronica Wipes the Face of Jesus

Background: The Catholic Encyclopedia of 1913 ties this Veronica story to the best-known image of Christ, the "true image" or "vera icon." Although this event is not in the Bible, Veronica's compassion in action for the suffering is a lesson we can all emulate, understanding that even our least action for the Lord is important (Matthew 25:40).

Location to Search: This sixth station is found by turning from Al-Wad St (or El Wad Rd) onto Via Dolorosa (or Al Alam). Here, smaller unmarked shops prevail, so the best way to find the station is by searching these coordinates: 31.7794202, 35.231477

Note the words on the left door in steel, "VI Station"

Other Points of Interest: Mark Twain in his book *The Innocents Abroad*, writes how they knew the Veronica story to be true: "We knew this, because we saw this handkerchief in a cathedral in Paris, in another in Spain, and in two others in Italy. In the Milan cathedral it costs five francs to see it, and at St. Peter's, at Rome, it is almost impossible to see it at any price. No tradition is so amply verified as this of St. Veronica and her handkerchief."

A place with true biblical events to explore with many pictures is the "Garden of Gethsemane, Jerusalem" where Jesus spent His last free moments in prayer.

SEVENTH STATION

Jesus Falls the Second Time

V. We adore Thee, O Christ, and we praise Thee, *(Genuflect)*
R. Because by Thy holy cross Thou hast redeemed the world. *(Rise)*

Priest:

CONSIDER the second fall of Jesus under the cross — a fall which renews the pains of all the wounds of the head and members of our afflicted Lord. *(Kneel)*

All Say:

MY MOST GENTLE JESUS, * how many times Thou hast pardoned me, * and how many times have I fallen again, and begun again to offend Thee! * Oh, by the merits of this new fall, * give me the necessary help to persevere in Thy grace until death. * Grant that in all temptations which assail me * I may always commend myself to Thee. I love Thee, Jesus, my love, with my whole heart; * I repent of having offended Thee. * Never permit me to offend Thee again. * Grant that I may love Thee always, * and then do with me what Thou wilt. *

Our Father. Hail Mary. Glory Be.

V. Lord Jesus, crucified,
R. Have mercy on us!
(Rise)

Pro peccátis suæ gentis	*Bruised, derided, cursed, defiled,*
Vidit Jésum in torméntis,	*She beheld her tender child,*
Et flagéllis súbditum.	*All with bloody scourges rent.*

Seventh Station Map Tourist
Jesus Falls the Second Time

Background: Jesus is brought low again (Psalm 38:6). This seventh station is at the main crossroad's arch built during Hadrian's reign (117-138 AD). Tradition adds that the death sentence of Jesus was posted here, hence the arch became known as the Judgement Gate. The arch's column can be seen inside the Franciscan chapel located inside the doors of this location.

Location to Search: The seventh station is posted above the door to a Franciscan chapel. The chapel is unmarked and is opened only while the Franciscans weekly walk the stations of the cross. An easy way to find this seventh station is by searching these coordinates: 31.7793963, 35.2308792

Other Points of Interest: Old Jerusalem is divided by religion into four quarters along the streets of the Gates of the Old City. These gates have a history of their own, and exploring them provides greater depth to the lives of the past. Searchers can look up Lion's Gate (exiting to Gethsemane), Jaffa Gate, or even the Dung Gate.

This seventh station is the last in the Muslim quarter of Old Jerusalem, and the next station is inside the Christian quarter.

EIGHTH STATION

The Women of Jerusalem Weep Over Jesus

V. We adore Thee, O Christ, and we praise Thee, *(Genuflect)*
R. Because by Thy holy cross Thou hast redeemed the world. *(Rise)*

Priest:

CONSIDER THAT those women wept with compassion at seeing Jesus in so pitiable a state, streaming with blood, as He walked along. But Jesus said to them, "Weep not for Me, but for your children." *(Kneel)*

All Say:

MY JESUS, * laden with sorrows, I weep for the offenses that I have committed against Thee, * because of the pains which they have deserved, * and still more because of the displeasure which they have caused Thee, * Who hast loved me so much. * It is Thy love, more than the fear of Hell, * which causes me to weep for my sins. * My Jesus, I love Thee more than myself; * I repent of having offended Thee. * Never permit me to offend Thee again. * Grant that I may love Thee always, * and then do with me what Thou wilt. *

Our Father. Hail Mary. Glory Be.

V. Lord Jesus, crucified,
R. Have mercy on us!
(Rise)

Vidit suum dulcem natum	*For the sins of His own nation*
Moriéndo, desolátum,	*Saw Him hang in desolation,*
Dum emísit spíritum.	*Till His spirit forth He sent.*

Eighth First Station Map Tourist
The Women of Jerusalem Weep Over Jesus

Background: The women weeping for Jesus is from Luke 23:27, a fulfillment of Zecharia 12:10. Jesus responds to the women by telling them not to weep for Him, but weep for Jerusalem's future destruction in 70 AD, but they gave no sign of understanding His prediction. Also not understood by His followers is that they are just days away from His joyful resurrection, as He predicted in John 16:20, where their grief will turn to joy!

Location to Search: This eighth station location is on the back wall of a monastery, most easily found by searching these coordinates: 31.7791331, 35.2301692

Other Points of Interest: Below the eighth station marker is a round stone with the words IC XC NIKA carved around a cross, which signifies "Jesus Christ Conquers."

If you can't get enough of the local food, Amigo Emil Restaurant is just west with more interesting food in a more interesting building than the standard Via Dolorosa vendors.

The Jewish Temple wasn't completely destroyed by the Romans in 70 AD. The Western Wall is a major attraction today as the Temple's "Holy of Holies" (the inner sanctuary where God appeared) was behind this wall.

NINTH STATION

Jesus Falls the Third Time

V. We adore Thee, O Christ, and we praise Thee, *(Genuflect)*
R. Because by Thy holy cross Thou hast redeemed the world. *(Rise)*
Priest:

CONSIDER THE THIRD FALL of Jesus Christ. His weakness was extreme, and the cruelty of His executioners excessive, who tried to hasten His steps when He had scarcely the strength to move. *(Kneel)*

All Say:

AH, MY OUTRAGED JESUS, * by the merits of the weakness that Thou didst suffer in going to Calvary, * give me strength sufficient to conquer all human respect * and all my wicked passions, * which have led me to despise Thy friendship. * I love Thee, Jesus, my love, with my whole heart; * I repent of having offended Thee. * Never permit me to offend Thee again. * Grant that I may love Thee always, * and then do with me what Thou wilt. *

Our Father. Hail Mary. Glory Be.

V. Lord Jesus, crucified,
R. Have mercy on us!
(Rise)

Eia, Mater, fons amóris	*O thou Mother! fount of love,*
Me sentíre vim dolóris.	*Touch my spirit from above,*
Fac, ut tecum lúgeam.	*Make my heart with thine accord.*

Ninth Station Map Tourist
Jesus Falls the Third Time

Background: Tradition holds that Jesus fell for a third time at this ninth station. Though Jesus has fallen, God gives strength to Him and us (Psalm 37:24) as we walk in His ways (1 Kings 3:14).

Location to Search: This ninth station sign is on an alley leading to the "Coptic Orthodox Patriarchate Jerusalem", or search these coordinates: 31.7788137, 35.2302711

Other Points of Interest: From this alley of the Coptic Church one can see the dome and cross on the Church of the Holy Sepulchre, the location of the next four stations.

An area to visit outside Old Jerusalem is the Jerusalem Botanical Gardens. It contains many of the plants and trees identified in the Bible. Their Bible Path tour includes Hyssop, Cedars of Lebanon, and many ceremonial plants.

TENTH STATION

Jesus Is Stripped of His Garments

V. We adore Thee, O Christ, and we praise Thee, *(Genuflect)*
R. Because by Thy holy cross Thou hast redeemed the world. *(Rise)*

Priest:

CONSIDER THE VIOLENCE with which the executioners stripped Jesus. His inner garments adhered to His torn flesh, and they dragged them off so roughly that the skin came with them. Compassionate your Savior thus cruelly treated, and say to Him: *(Kneel)*

All Say:

MY INNOCENT JESUS, * by the merits of the torment which Thou hast felt, * help me to strip myself of all affection to things of earth, * in order that I may place all my love in Thee. * Who art so worthy of my love. * I love Thee, O Jesus, with my whole heart; * I repent of having offended Thee. * Never permit me to offend Thee again. * Grant that I may love Thee always, * and then do with me what Thou wilt. *

Our Father. Hail Mary. Glory Be.

V. Lord Jesus, crucified,
R. Have mercy on us!
(Rise)

Fac, ut árdeat cor meum	*Make me feel as thou hast felt;*
In amándo Christum Deum,	*Make my soul to glow and melt*
Ut sibi compláceam.	*With the love of Christ, my Lord.*

Tenth First Station Map Tourist

Jesus Is Stripped of His Garments

Background: This tenth station commemorates when Jesus had His clothing removed and soldiers cast lots for them (Matt. 27:35, Mark 15:24, Luke 23:34, John 19:24), fulfilling Psalm 22:18. We too will leave this earth without possession, so let us build treasures in heaven (Matt. 6:20).

In the year 326, Constantine the Great sent his mother Helena to find Golgotha (Calvary) and Christ's tomb. She found one of three crosses that people attributed to miraculous healing and a tomb cut from the rock. It is here that the Church of the Holy Sepulchre was constructed.

Location to Search: This tenth station is inside the Church of the Holy Sepulchre and thus has no specific pinpoint map location. The tenth station can be seen searching for the blue-domed "Chapel of the Franks", which is part of the greater Church. Chapel history, images, and videos can be found online. The Church can be found by searching with these coordinates: 31.7783694, 35.2296889

Other Points of Interest: The soldiers likely wanted to sell the clothes of Jesus, as they had value. You can get some of the coins used in the time of Jesus, touching the past, by getting your own denarius on auction sites, or even a widow's mite from Mark 12:42, both 2,000 years old for under $50 each.

ELEVENTH STATION

Jesus Is Nailed to The Cross

V. We adore Thee, O Christ, and we praise Thee, *(Genuflect)*
R. Because by Thy holy cross Thou hast redeemed the world. *(Rise)*

Priest:

CONSIDER THAT JESUS, after being thrown on the cross, extended His hands, and offered to His eternal Father the sacrifice of His life for our salvation. These barbarians fastened Him with nails, and then, raising the cross, left Him to die with anguish on this infamous gibbet. *(Kneel)*

All Say:

MY JESUS, loaded with contempt, * nail my heart to Thy feet, that it may ever remain there * to love Thee and never quit Thee again. * I love Thee more than myself; * I repent of having offended Thee. * Never permit me to offend Thee again. * Grant that I may love Thee always, * and then do with me what Thou wilt. *

Our Father. Hail Mary. Glory Be.

V. Lord Jesus, crucified,
R. Have mercy on us!
(Rise)

Sancta Mater istud ages,	*Holy Mother, pierce me through!*
Crucifíxi fige plagas	*In my heart each wound renew*
Cordi meo válide.	*Of my Savior crucified.*

Eleventh Station Map Tourist
Jesus Is Nailed to The Cross

Background: This sorrowful event of Luke 23:33 was for us. Our sins and problems were nailed to the cross, the task complete, the action done. No more do we need to live in darkness, as Jesus came for this moment on the cross and His resurrection, to set us free forevermore (Rom. 8:2).

Location to Search: This eleventh station is inside the Church of the Holy Sepulchre and thus has no specific pinpoint map location. The eleventh station can be seen searching for the "Chapel of the Nails of the Cross", which is inside the Church. Chapel of the Nails history, images, and videos can be found online. The Church can be found by searching with these coordinates: 31.7783694, 35.2296889

Other Points of Interest: Jerusalem has had a permanent civilization for over 3,000 years in a troubled area (it has been attacked over 52 times). To see what Jerusalem looked like during the time of Jesus, one way to do that is visit the half acre "Second Temple Jerusalem Model" at the "Israel Museum". It features sites in 1:50 scale mentioned throughout the Bible, like Herod's Palace (Acts 23:35) and Pool of Bethesda (John 5:2), bringing their glory to life.

TWELFTH STATION

Jesus Is Raised Upon the Cross and Dies

V. We adore Thee, O Christ, and we praise Thee, *(Genuflect)*
R. Because by Thy holy cross Thou hast redeemed the world. *(Rise)*

Priest:

CONSIDER HOW THY JESUS, after three hours of agony on the cross, consumed at length with anguish, abandons Himself to the weight of His body, bows His head, and dies. *(Kneel)*

All Say:

O MY DYING JESUS, * I kiss devoutly the cross on which Thou didst die for love of me. * I have merited by my sins to die a miserable death, * but Thy death is my hope. * Ah, by the merits of Thy death, * give me the grace to die, embracing Thy feet * and burning with love for Thee. * I commit my soul into Thy hands. * I love Thee with my whole heart; * I repent of ever having offended Thee. * Never permit me to offend Thee again. * Grant that I may love Thee always, * and then do with me what Thou wilt. *

Our Father. Hail Mary. Glory Be.

V. Lord Jesus, crucified,
R. Have mercy on us!
(Rise)

Tui nati vulneráti,
Tam dignáti pro me pati,
Poenas pomecum dívide.

Let me share with thee His pain,
Who for all our sins was slain,
Who for me in torments died.

Twelfth Station Map Tourist
Jesus Is Raised Upon the Cross and Dies

Background: Here is commemorated where Jesus gave up His spirit (Matt. 27:50), so that the work He came to complete would be finished (John 19:30). From this act beyond comprehension, we have been made holy through Jesus (Heb. 10:10), to live in Him (John 15:5), and be His love here on earth (Eph. 5:2).

Location to Search: This twelfth station is inside the Church of the Holy Sepulchre, found by searching for the "Altar of the Crucifixion Holy Sepulchre". The Altar is built on Golgotha rock, where visitors are permitted to kneel and touch the spot believed to be where the cross of Jesus stood. Altar images and videos are online. The Church can be found by searching with these coordinates: 31.7783694, 35.2296889

Other Points of Interest: Seeing is believing at the Tisch Family Zoological Gardens, where one can see many biblical animals on display, like the oryx (Deut. 33:17), tortoise (Lev. 11:29), and the addax (Deut. 14:5).

THIRTEENTH STATION

Jesus Is Taken Down from The Cross and Placed in The Arms of His Mother

V. We adore Thee, O Christ, and we praise Thee, *(Genuflect)*
R. Because by Thy holy cross Thou hast redeemed the world. *(Rise)*

Priest:

CONSIDER THAT Our Lord having expired, two of His disciples, Joseph and Nicodemus, took Him down from the cross and placed Him in the arms of His afflicted Mother, who received Him with unutterable tenderness and pressed Him to her bosom. *(Kneel)*

All Say:

O MOTHER OF SORROWS, * for the love of this Son, * accept me for thy servant, * and pray to Him for me. * And Thou, my Redeemer, * since Thou hast died for me, * permit me to love Thee; * for I wish but Thee, my Jesus, * and I repent of ever having offended Thee. * Never permit me to offend Thee again. * Grant that I may love Thee always, * and then do with me what Thou wilt. *

Our Father. Hail Mary. Glory Be.

V. Lord Jesus, crucified,
R. Have mercy on us!
(Rise)

Fac me tecum pie flere,	*Let me mingle tears with thee*
Crucifíxo condolére,	*Mourning Him who mourned for me,*
Donec ego víxero.	*All the days that I may live.*

Thirteenth Station Map Tourist
Jesus Is Taken Down from The Cross and
Placed in The Arms of His Mother

Background: The world may rejoice at unrighteousness (Luke 23:48), but it is Mary in whom we rejoice, showing true love administering to the needs of Jesus (Mark 15:41).

Jesus was taken down from the cross by Joseph of Arimathea and Nicodemus, both part of the Jewish order and secretly disciples of Jesus (John 19:38). They performed a proper Jewish burial, anointing the body of Jesus with 75 pounds of myrrh and aloe, and wrapping Him in white linen.

Location to Search: The thirteenth station is inside the Church of the Holy Sepulchre and thus has no specific pinpoint map location. The thirteenth station can be seen searching for the "stone of anointing at the Church of the Holy Sepulchre". Images and videos are online. The Church can be found by searching with these coordinates: 31.7783694, 35.2296889

Other Points of Interest: The Holy Sepulchre has many more interesting attractions. Searching image results for the "floor plan of the Holy Sepulchre" will name and place the 30 plus chapels and worship spaces from which to explore further. Or, searching for a "video tour inside the Holy Sepulchre" will result in many step-by-step walkthrough videos posted by both tourists and tour guides.

FOURTEENTH STATION

Jesus Is Laid in The Sepulcher

V. We adore Thee, O Christ, and we praise Thee, *(Genuflect)*
R. Because by Thy holy cross Thou hast redeemed the world. *(Rise)*

Priest:

CONSIDER THAT the disciples carried the body of Jesus to bury it, accompanied by His holy Mother, who arranged it in the sepulcher with her own hands. They then closed the tomb, and all withdrew. *(Kneel)*

All Say:

AH, MY BURIED JESUS, * I kiss the stone that encloses Thee. * But Thou didst rise again the third day. * I beseech Thee, by Thy resurrection, * make me rise glorious with Thee at The Last Day, * to be always united with Thee in Heaven, * to praise Thee and love Thee forever. * I love Thee, * and I repent of ever having offended Thee. * Never permit me to offend Thee again. * Grant that I may love Thee always, * and then do with me what Thou wilt. *

Our Father. Hail Mary. Glory Be.

V. Lord Jesus, crucified,
R. Have mercy on us!
(Rise)

Juxta crucem tecum stare,	*By the cross with thee to stay,*
Et me tibi sociáre,	*There with thee to weep and pray,*
In planctu desídero.	*Is all I ask of thee to give.*

Fourteenth Station Map Tourist
Jesus Is Laid in The Sepulcher

Background: At the place where He was crucified, there was a garden and tomb (John 19:41). It was in this tomb that the body of Jesus was placed on the hewn slab, as it was nearby and the sabbath was about to start.

The fourteenth station is the tomb where Jesus was lain, now covered with an aedicule (shrine). The first aedicule was built in the eleventh century by the Crusaders, which placed a protective stone above the slab where Jesus was lain. By 1555 a second protective stone was placed to enclose both stones, so visitors can "kiss the stone that encloses Thee."

Location to Search: The fourteenth station is inside the Church of the Holy Sepulchre and thus has no specific pinpoint map location. The fourteenth station can be seen searching for the "Aedicule Tomb of Jesus". Images and videos are online. The Church can be found by searching with these coordinates: 31.7783694, 35.2296889

Other Points of Interest: Praise the Lord this fourteenth station is not the end of the story, for He has risen (Matt. 28:6), was carried to heaven (Luke 24:51), and will come back (Rev. 1:7)!

His ascension is believed to have been near the Mount of Olives, found by searching the Chapel of the Ascension, Jerusalem.

After this, return to the high altar and, to complete the devotion, say the Our Father, Hail Mary, *and* Glory Be *five times in honor of the Passion of Jesus Christ.*

PRAYER TO JESUS CHRIST CRUCIFIED

Behold, O kind and most sweet Jesus, * I cast myself upon my knees in Thy sight, * and with the most fervent desire of my soul, * I pray and beseech Thee that Thou wouldst impress upon my heart * lively sentiments of faith, hope and charity, * with true contrition for my sins * and with a firm purpose of amendment; * while with deep affection and grief of soul, * I ponder within my self and mentally contemplate Thy five wounds, * having before my eyes the words which David the prophet * put on Thy lips concerning Thee: * "They have pierced My hands and My feet, * they have numbered all My bones."

At the end, one Our Father *and* Hail Mary, *at least, should be said for the intention of the Sovereign Pontiff; this will fulfill the requirements for a plenary indulgence connected to this devotion — so long as a person also fulfills the other requirements.*

SABAT MATER

Virgo virginum praeclara
Mihi jam non sis amara
Fac me tecum plangere;

Fac, et portem Christi mortem,
Passionis fac consortem,
Et plagas recolere.

Fac me plagis vulnerary,
Fac me cruce inebriari,
Et cruore Filii.

Flammis ne urar succensus
Per te, Virgo, sim defensus
In die judicii.

Christe, cum sit hinc exire,
Da per Matrem me venire
Ad palmam victoriae.

Quando corpus morietur,
Fac ut animae donetur
Paradisi gloria. Amen.

V. Ora pro nobis, Virgo dolorosissima.
R. Ut digni efficiamur promisionibus Christi.

Virgin of all virgins blest!
Listen to my fond request:
Let me share thy grief divine;

Let me, to my latest breath,
In my body bear the death
Of that dying Son of thine.

Wounded with His every wound,
Steep my soul till it hath swooned
In His very Blood away.

Be to me, O Virgin, nigh,
Lest in flames I burn and die,
In His awful Judgement Day.

Christ, when Thou shalt call me hence,
Be Thy Mother my defense,
Be Thy cross my victory.

While my body here decays,
May my soul Thy goodness praise,
Safe in paradise with Thee. Amen

V. Pray for us, Virgin most sorrowful.
R. That we may be made worthy of the promises of Christ.

INDULGENCES

A Plenary indulgence is granted to the faithful who make the pious exercise of the Way of the Cross. Those who are impeded can gain the same indulgence if they spend at least one half an hour in pious reading and meditation on the Passion and Death of our Lord Jesus Christ.

Enchiridion Indulgentiarum, no. 63

www.ingramcontent.com/pod-product-compliance
Lightning Source LLC
Chambersburg PA
CBHW061212070526
44583CB00025B/3223